ENERGY

by John Stringer

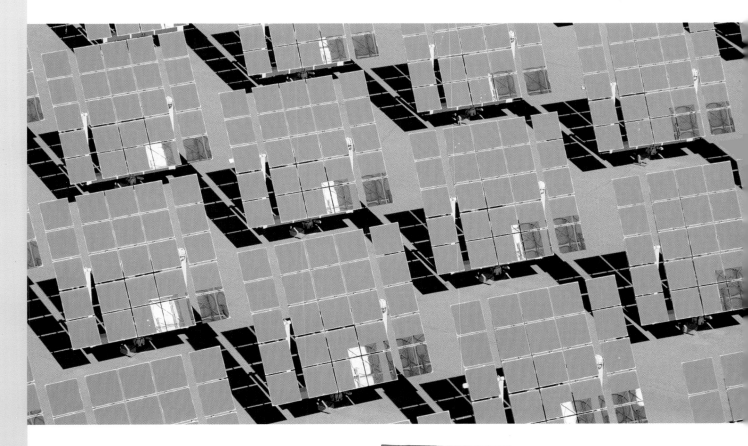

Evans

WWF

VISIT OUR WEBSITE
www.evansbooks.co.uk

Published by Evans Brothers Limited
2A Portman Mansions
Chiltern Street,
London W1U 6NR

© White-Thomson Publishing Ltd 2006

Produced for Evans Brothers Limited by

White-Thomson Publishing Ltd
210 High Street,
Lewes, East Sussex
BN7 2NH

Editorial: Clare Collinson and Catherine Clarke
Design: Tinstar Design Ltd (www.tinstar.co.uk)
Consultant: Mike Wolfe
WWF reviewers: Patricia Kendell and Cherry Duggan
Picture research: Amy Sparks

The publishers would like to thank Sally Morgan for
her assistance with the preparation of this book.

Printed in China by WKT on chlorine-free paper
from sustainably managed forests.

**British Library Cataloguing
in Publication Data.**

Stringer, John
    Energy. - (Sustainable futures)
    1. Power resources - Juvenile literature
    2. Energy consumption - Juvenile literature
    3. Sustainable development - Juvenile literature
    I. Title
    333.7'917

    ISBN-13: 9780237527624
    ISBN-10: 0237527626

WWF and the Sustainable Futures series

There are many environmental problems facing
our planet, but there is much that we can all do
to improve the situation.

WWF works to save endangered species, protect
endangered spaces and address global threats to
nature such as climate change. That is why we are
happy to be associated with the "Sustainable Futures"
series, which offers information for you
to learn from, think about and act on. Your actions
will be crucial to the future of planet Earth.

WWF-UK Registered Charity No. 1081247. A
company limited by guarantee number 4016725.
Panda symbol © 1986 WWF. ® WWF Registered
trademark.

The views of the author expressed in this publication
do not necessarily reflect those of WWF.

The author has used all reasonable endeavours to
ensure that the content of this report, the data
compiled, and the methods of calculation and
research are consistent with normally accepted
standards and practices. However, no warranty is
given to that effect nor any liability accepted by the
authors for any loss or damage arising from the use of
this report by WWF-UK or by any other party.

For further information, please contact:

WWF-UK
Panda House, Weyside Park
Godalming, Surrey GU7 1XR
Telephone: 01483 426444
Fax: 01483 426409
http://www.wwf.org.uk

Acknowledgements

The publishers would like to thank the following for
permission to reproduce photographs:

Alamy **p. 37** (Agripicture Images); Corbis **pp. 6** (Roger
Ressmeye), **9** (Liu Liqun), **10** (China Photo/Reuters), **11**
(Ustinenko Anatoly/ITAR-TASS), **16** (Mark A. Johnson), **17**
(David Samuel Robbins), **20** (Dietrich Rose/zefa), **24** (Lester
Lefkowitz), **25** (Tom Bean), **28** (Raymond Gehman), **33**
(James L. Amos); Ecoscene **pp. 14** (Judyth Platt), **15** (John
Liddiard), **19** (Jim Winkley), **22** (Genevieve Leaper), **30** (Peter
Hulme), **35** (Joel Creed), **40** (Bruce Harber); The Image
Works (Anthony Robert La Penna/Bangor Daily News) **p. 44**;
JAMSTEC **p. 26**; Ocean Power Delivery Ltd **p. 27**;
photolibrary **pp. 5** (Index Stock Imagery), **12** (Digitalvision),
13 (Australia), **18** (Phototake Inc), **21** (Index Stock Imagery),
31 (Index Stock Imagery), **32** (Digitalvision), **39** (Index Stock
Imagery), **41** (Jon Arnold Images), **42** (Australia); Practical
Action ITDG/Neil Cooper **p. 8**; Science Photo Library (Tony
McConnell) **p. 38**; Topfoto **pp. 29, 23** (The Image Works),
45 (Jim West/The Image Works); Toyota Ltd (GB) **p. 43**;
uppa.co.uk/Mark Fairhurst **p. 36**; WTPix **pp. 4, 7, 34**.

Cover photograph reproduced with permission
of OSF/Photolibrary/Ifa-Bilderteam Gmbh.

Contents

CHAPTER 1

Energy in the 21st century

In August 2005 Hurricane Katrina swept across the Gulf of Mexico, destroying much in its path. Not only did the hurricane make millions of people homeless but it disrupted the supply of oil from the oilfields of the Gulf of Mexico, an area that supplies one third of the USA's oil needs. There were long queues at petrol stations in the USA as people rushed to buy fuel for their cars before the oil ran out. The disruption to the oil supply only lasted a week or so but the people of the southern states of the USA learnt what it would be like to live in a world where oil was in short supply.

Our energy needs

Experts predict that during the 21st century the world's demand for energy will more than double. In 2004 world energy consumption rose by 4.3 per cent – the largest-ever increase in energy consumption in one year. There is no reason to expect the demand for energy to slow down. As more countries around the world become industrialised and their living standards improve, more and more energy is needed. For example, the economy of China has been growing so fast that the country's energy needs can no longer be met by its own energy resources. The consumption of energy in China grew by 65 per cent between 2001 and 2004.

Large cities such as Hong Kong make huge demands on the Earth's energy resources. Most of the energy used to power the city's lights comes from power stations that use non-renewable fuels to generate electricity.

Non-renewable energy

At present, most of the world's energy comes from non-renewable fossil fuels – oil, coal and natural gas. Fossil fuels cannot be replaced as fast as they are being used so they will eventually run out. Experts estimate that the world's oil will last for another 40 years and that its natural gas will last for 65 years. Coal might last 160 years. As fossil fuels become more scarce and valuable, so the cost of these fuels rises. The use of fossil fuels for energy also has a harmful effect on the environment. Environmental damage is created at every stage of extracting, processing and using these fuels. When fossil fuels are burnt they produce carbon dioxide and other polluting gases, causing global warming and acid rain.

The switch to renewable energy

An alternative to burning fossil fuels is to use renewable sources of energy such as wood, wind, Sun and water power. When these sources of energy are used they are continually replenished, so they will not run out. Renewable sources of energy are already important in some countries. For example, Norway has high mountains and plenty of rivers, so the country generates nine-tenths of its electricity from hydroelectric schemes, which harness the power of moving water to generate energy. In the US state of California, solar energy, in the form of heat and light from the Sun, is used to provide power for a million homes. Many countries, including Denmark, Portugal, Spain, Germany and the UK use wind power for some of their energy needs.

A sustainable future?

The word 'sustainability' means 'the ability to continue to support itself indefinitely'. Therefore an energy source can be considered to be sustainable if it is continually replenished and can be used by future generations. The switch to renewable energy sources is vital if the world's resources are to be used in a sustainable way.

Wind is a renewable source of energy that can be used to turn wind turbines that generate electricity.

Energy facts

▶ Total fossil-fuel use in the USA has increased twenty-fold in the last four decades.

▶ The USA uses between 20 and 30 times more fossil fuel energy per person than people in developing nations.

▶ More than half the world's electricity is generated using coal. This burns 1.9 billion tons of coal each year.

Nuclear power

Uranium is a metal that is mined in many parts of the world. In 1937 two German scientists discovered that they could release huge amounts of energy if they split atoms of this radioactive element. The reaction, called nuclear fission, can be controlled in power station reactors and used to make electricity. Nuclear power produces around 16 per cent of the world's electricity needs, at about the same cost as energy from coal. It produces huge amounts of energy from small amounts of fuel. But is it sustainable and is it safe?

Unlike fossil fuels, nuclear power does not produce smoke or carbon dioxide. However, it is a non-renewable source of energy, because once we have mined all of the world's uranium there will not be any more to replace it. Nuclear power stations produce radioactive waste, which is dangerous to transport and store. The waste has to be sealed up for hundreds of years until the radioactivity has fallen to safe levels. There are also concerns about the safety of nuclear power plants. Accidents can cause dangerous radiation to escape and pollute the surrounding land and air, so the processes in nuclear plants need to be carefully monitored.

"Because electricity produced from nuclear sources generates none of the greenhouse gases associated with burning fossil fuels, nuclear power makes a substantial contribution to limiting such emissions."

The Energy Report 1999, UK Department of Trade and Industry

Opponents of the Three Mile Island nuclear plant in the USA say that people are forgetting the lessons of the accident that occurred there in 1979.

"I think people have short memories. I think the issue is not if we'll have another accident, but when."

Eric J. Epstein, Three Mile Island Alert, an organisation that opposes the Three Mile Island nuclear plant

Paluel Nuclear Plant on the Normandy coast is one of 22 nuclear power plants in France. Nuclear and hydroelectric power supply 90 per cent of the country's electricity.

There have been two major nuclear power station disasters, one at Three Mile Island in the USA in 1979 and the other at Chernobyl in the former Soviet Union in 1986. However, stringent precautions are taken to prevent accidents. Countries such as the UK, Canada, the USA and Russia make use of nuclear energy, while France, Finland and Sweden depend heavily on nuclear power. In recent years, a number of countries such as the UK and the USA have been reducing their use of nuclear power. However, these countries may have to review their policy as oil and gas become more expensive and as reducing carbon dioxide emissions is seen as more important.

Demand for energy

Industrialised countries such as the USA, Germany, Japan and the UK use many times the amount of energy used by less industrialised countries such as Kenya or Ethiopia. Out of the world's population, one person in twenty is an American. You might expect that the USA would consume one-twentieth of the world's energy, but it currently uses one-third of global energy. Each person living in the USA uses the equivalent of 7800 tons of oil in their lifetime. In comparison, in Ethiopia the energy use per head is equivalent to 28 tons of oil. As the industrialised countries of the West become more and more wealthy, their consumption of energy increases.

There is also a huge rise in demand for energy in countries with rapidly growing economies such as China and India. In India, for example, there are increasing demands for services such as air conditioning. These demands cannot be met from India's own resources. India relies on coal for more than half of its energy needs, to fuel its factories and transport. Although it is the world's third largest producer of coal, with 300,000 coal mines, India cannot maintain its economic growth without new energy sources.

Saving energy

There is a lot of wastage of energy. People leave computers and televisions on standby and this uses up electricity. Cities are lit up at night with street lighting and advertising. Cars burn fuel when they stand idle in traffic jams and when they wait at traffic lights.

There are many easy ways to save energy such as switching off equipment and lights when they are not in use, using low-energy light bulbs, insulating the home to reduce heat loss and turning off the car engine when the car is not moving. Reducing the demand for electricity means that less fuel is burnt by power stations.

Cities across the world are becoming clogged with energy-demanding traffic. These vehicles in Mumbai, India, are burning fossil fuels and producing polluting gases. As the standard of living rises in India more people are able to afford a car.

Improved cooking stoves, such as this one being used in Kenya, have made dramatic savings in energy.

Developing countries

In many developing countries an electricity supply is a luxury. Often these countries are too poor to be able to build coal- or oil-burning power stations. However, as these countries have started to develop their industries and their populations have grown, the need for energy has increased.

Many people in developing countries rely on wood as their main source of energy. Wood is collected and burnt on wood-burning stoves for cooking and heating. As the demand for energy has increased, more wood is being collected. The forests are being cleared more quickly than new trees can grow, so this use of wood is not sustainable. There are environmental problems, too. When the trees are cleared, the soil surrounding the roots is left exposed to the wind and rain. As a result, the soil is blown or washed away. This is called soil erosion. Once the soil has been eroded, little can be grown on the land.

Improving sustainability

Now some non-governmental organisations, such as the Intermediate Technology Development Group (ITDG), are working closely with communities in developing countries such as Kenya and Nepal to introduce stoves that are more efficient and require less wood than traditional stoves. For example, in 1998 the ITDG worked with people in Turkana, Kenya, to develop a new kind of stove with a thick clay liner. The lining of the stove conserves heat – making it more energy-efficient. Following the introduction of these stoves, fewer trees have been cut down, more trees have been allowed to grow to maturity and the fuel source has become sustainable.

Case Study: The Three Gorges Dam

In the past few years, China has undergone rapid industrialisation and the demand for energy has increased. Today, most of China's energy needs are met by burning coal, but a new hydroelectric dam is being built on the longest river in China, the River Yangtze. It will produce one-eighth of China's energy needs and save 45 million tons of coal a year. When the Three Gorges Dam is completed in 2009, it will be 2 kilometres long and 185 metres high. Behind it is a 600-kilometre-wide lake.

Although the Three Gorges Dam will have huge benefits in terms of cheap energy for industry, the construction of the dam is having a damaging impact on the environment and it is forcing many people to move their homes. Around 2 million people will have to find new homes and unknown numbers of animals will lose their habitat. Among these animals is a fish called the Chinese sturgeon, known as 'the panda of the water' because – like the panda – it is endangered. Environmentalists are concerned that the changes to its habitat could drive the sturgeon to extinction.

The construction site of the Three Gorges Dam is huge. The hydroelectric plant in the dam will be the largest in the world.

Fossil fuels

Coal, oil and natural gas are fossil fuels which come from within the Earth. These fuels provide the energy used in the world today for cooking, heating, lighting, generating electricity and running vehicles. But supplies of these fuels are limited and they are not being replaced as fast as they are being used. This means that these fuels are not sustainable – one day they will run out.

How do fossil fuels form?

Plants are able to make their own food using a process called photosynthesis, which harnesses energy from sunlight. The energy they capture cannot be destroyed. It remains locked up in the remains of the plants even after they die and rot away.

Fossil fuels were formed from tiny plants and animals that lived millions of years ago. Coal is made from the remains of plants. Oil and natural gas were formed when marine organisms died and sank to the bottom of the sea. Gradually, layers of sand and mud built up and over millions of years the remains of the organisms became part of the Earth's rock. Pressure, temperature and chemical conditions eventually converted them to oil and gas. When fossil fuels are burnt the energy they contain is released.

Oil

Oil is a fossil fuel that is essential to the modern world. As well as providing fuel for most of the world's road transport, oil is used in the manufacture of products including plastic, which has replaced many natural materials. The oil industry is big business, generating huge amounts of money each year. Of the top fourteen highest earning companies in the USA, eight are in the petroleum industry. Worldwide we use around 3.5 billion tons of oil a year and in 2005, oil production was at 2.5 million barrels a day. (A barrel of oil is 159 litres.)

Action is already being taken to reduce oil use in Europe and North America. Cars and other road vehicles are becoming more efficient and alternative fuels such as biodiesel are replacing oil.

These plastic bottles in China are going to be recycled. Plastic is an oil product and some people argue that plastic bottles should be burnt, like any other oil product, to produce energy. However, care would have to be taken that toxic products of the burning process did not escape into the atmosphere.

Case Study: The Caspian Sea

The Caspian Sea in central Asia is a land-locked sea surrounded by five countries: Iran, Turkmenistan, Kazakhstan, Russia and Azerbaijan. There is a huge oilfield lying under the Caspian Sea, with reserves estimated at between 50 and 100 billion barrels. In comparison, the USA has known reserves of 21 billion barrels, while the North Sea field to the north-east of the UK contains about 16 billion barrels.

Kazakhstan owns the largest proportion of the oil reserves in the Caspian Sea but it has problems getting the oil to markets in Europe and other parts of Asia. To reach these markets, the oil has to be piped underground either to a terminal on the Black Sea where it can be transferred into oil tankers, which transport the oil by sea, or piped directly west to the markets in Europe or south into Asia. One pipeline to the west is currently under construction and when complete it will be able to carry 1 million barrels a day from Kazakhstan to the Black Sea. The construction is a mammoth project as the pipeline crosses mountainous regions that are prone to earthquakes. There is also considerable political unrest and the threat of terrorist attacks in the countries through which the pipeline is being built, including Iraq, Iran and Afghanistan.

New oilfields are being discovered in the Caspian Sea. This oil rig is digging an exploratory well.

Oil refining

Crude oil extracted from the ground is a mixture of chemical compounds made up of carbon and hydrogen. These compounds are known as hydrocarbons. We cannot use crude oil in its natural state, but when the different compounds in the mixture are separated we can obtain many useful fuels. The compounds are separated in oil refineries by a process called fractional distillation.

Some of the products of the fractionating process are used as fuels such as petrol, diesel and paraffin. Others are used for lubrication, for road surfaces and for roofing. Some of the oil is 'cracked', which means its molecules are broken up into smaller molecules. Other molecules are joined together into long chains. This is called polymerisation. Cracking and polymerisation produce plastics.

A typical coal-fired plant sends about twice the amount of carbon dioxide into the air as a plant that uses natural gas. Using coal as fuel also produces mercury, which settles in lakes and rivers and harms aquatic life.

Coal

Coal is a fossil fuel that was created over millions of years from the remains of dead plants, especially trees. When the coal is burnt, the chemical energy stored in the coal is converted to heat energy, which can be used to generate steam and produce electricity.

Many power stations around the world still burn fossil fuels such as coal. The coal is burnt in giant furnaces to heat water to make steam. The steam is piped through huge machines called turbines. The turbines turn great magnets inside coils of wire, generating electricity. The largest coal-fired power station in Europe is Drax in Yorkshire, UK. It produces 4000 megawatts of power, which is enough to supply electricity for about four million homes. It uses 36,000 tons of coal a day. The coal is delivered by trains straight from coal mines, each train carrying 1000 tons.

This open-cast coal mine in Australia is a huge hole in the ground. Open mines such as these scar the countryside and leave surfaces that are easily eroded by rain.

Coal mining

Almost all the world's coal comes from within the Earth. Coal mining can be harmful to the environment. It involves drilling a network of underground tunnels or digging a huge pit and it produces huge amounts of waste called slag. When a mine has been worked out and the miners have left, great scars and slag heaps are left behind. These sites can be restored by seeding grass and planting trees and this creates new wildlife habitats. However, the restoration process can be expensive, so in some countries the process is left to nature, which takes much longer.

Natural gas

Natural gas is a fossil fuel that was formed from the remains of microscopic plants and animals, just like oil. Natural gas is a mixture of the flammable gases methane, ethane, propane and butane. It is found trapped in the rock within the Earth, often above oil. Many of these rocks are under the sea and the gas is transported through pipes to homes and industry. Sometimes the gas is compressed so that it can be bottled. Natural gas is a valuable fuel and can be used to generate electricity. In many countries there has been a switch from coal-fired to gas-fired power stations because the combustion of gas produces far less carbon dioxide than the burning of coal. However, natural gas is not sustainable and the world's natural gas reserves may last for just 65 more years.

Fossil fuels and air pollution

When a hydrocarbon is burnt in air it releases carbon dioxide and water. However, fuels such as coal and oil are not pure hydrocarbons – they contain other substances, too. For example, coal contains sulphur. When coal is burnt, the sulphur reacts with air to form sulphur dioxide, one of the chemicals that causes acid rain.

Acid rain

Coal-fired power stations release sulphur dioxide, especially those burning lignite, a poor quality coal. This gas reacts with water in the air to form a weak acid. This creates acid rain – rain that has a lower pH than normal rain. Acid rain harms trees and lakes and damages buildings by eroding the stone from which they are made.

Acid rain has killed the trees that lie downwind from this coal-fired power station.

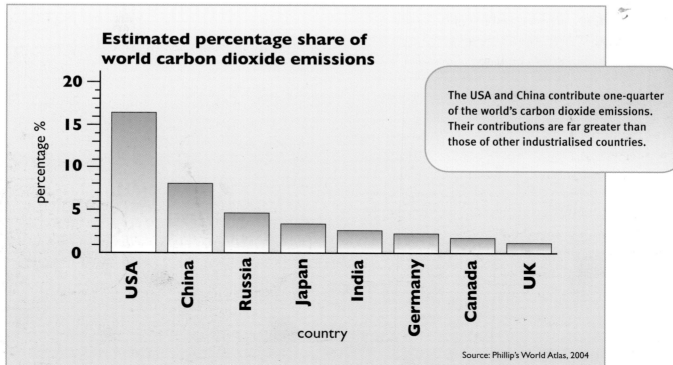

Estimated percentage share of world carbon dioxide emissions

The USA and China contribute one-quarter of the world's carbon dioxide emissions. Their contributions are far greater than those of other industrialised countries.

Source: Phillip's World Atlas, 2004

Acid rain falling on conifer forests of Scandinavia, Central Europe and North America has caused considerable damage. Huge numbers of trees have died, leaving the slopes bare. The acid drains through the soil and into rivers and lakes. As the water in lakes becomes more acidic, fish and other aquatic organisms die.

Nowadays, power stations in Europe and North America have to meet stringent regulations regarding their emissions of sulphur dioxide and they have fitted filters in the chimneys to absorb all the sulphur. However, regulations in other parts of the world are not quite so tough.

Global warming

Burning fossil fuels and wood releases carbon dioxide. Carbon dioxide is described as a greenhouse gas because it traps heat in the atmosphere. A natural blanket of greenhouse gases, including water vapour, carbon dioxide and methane, surrounds the Earth. These gases trap heat that is vital for life on Earth. Without this heat, Earth would become a frozen, lifeless planet. However, as more greenhouse gases are released into the atmosphere, more heat is trapped. The effect of this is a rise in the average global temperature of the Earth's surface. The rise could be as much as 3.5°C by the end of this century.

The effects of global warming are uncertain. However, it is likely that the rise in temperature will disrupt climates around the world, causing some areas to have more rain than before, others to have less. There could also be more extreme weather events, such as hurricanes, flooding and droughts. The increased temperatures are melting the ice sheets in the Arctic and Antarctica and this, combined with the expansion of water in the oceans, is causing the sea levels to rise.

Sea levels have already risen between 10 centimetres and 25 centimetres in the last 100 years. Low-lying land is being flooded. In 1988, the highest flood ever recorded occurred in Bangladesh when much of the country was left under water.

Climate change is warming the seas. Coral reefs are particularly sensitive to the slightest change in temperature. One sign of warmer water is the bleaching of corals. This fan coral is normally a bright red colour owing to the presence of tiny organisms that live with the coral, but they have been killed by the temperature change.

Renewable energy

Fossil fuels cannot provide energy for ever. As they start to run out, people will need to find ways of using more energy from renewable sources. Renewable energy is sustainable because it is constantly replaced, so it will not run out. People in developing countries already make good use of renewable resources such as wood. For example, about three billion people – half the world's population – burn wood to keep warm and for cooking. There are other renewable resources that offer a sustainable future, such as solar energy, wind and wave energy, energy from plant oils and even energy from waste.

Renewable energy sources

Renewable energy sources currently represent about 15 per cent of all energy use. Most of this comes from biofuels: wood, energy crops such as sugar cane, and biodiesel made from plant oils. Although solar energy and wind power are among the most familiar sources of renewable energy, they contribute just a couple of per cent. In time, however, as fossil fuels, especially oil, become more expensive, the proportion of our energy coming from renewable sources will increase and the proportion coming from fossil fuels will decrease.

Waves are a powerful source of renewable energy. This energy can be used to turn turbines and generate electricity.

Solar energy is a renewable source of energy that can be harnessed to provide heat. Solar kettles are used in many developing countries to heat water. The heat from these makeshift panels boils the water in the kettle.

Renewable energy – for and against

There are advantages and disadvantages to using renewable sources of energy. Solar, wind and water energy can be harnessed in many places around the world, including in developing countries. In contrast, fossil fuels tend to be found only in a few areas of the world. Oil, for example, is found mostly in the Middle East and North America. This makes countries without their own sources of fossil fuels dependent on other countries for their supply. Using renewable sources of energy makes these countries less dependent on oil-producing countries.

Most electricity tends to be generated by large, centralised power stations connected to a national grid that distributes the electricity. However, energy schemes that use renewable energy tend to be more localised, providing less expensive electricity for local communities. Generating electricity using renewable energy sources is currently more expensive than using oil, gas or coal, but advances in the efficiency of wind turbines and solar panels could change this.

The use of renewable energy sources to generate electricity does not result in the production of polluting gases that cause acid rain and global warming. However, harnessing water power through the construction of a dam can cause considerable damage to the ecology of a river and interferes with the flow of a river. The construction of wind farms also has an impact on the environment because it involves the building of new access roads and the digging of foundations for the turbines. No energy source is completely free of environmental damage so it is a question of balancing the benefits against the disadvantages.

"If humankind is going to have a future on this planet, at least a high-technology future, with a significant population of several billions of humans continuing to inhabit the Earth, it is absolutely inevitable that we'll have to find another energy source."

Professor Martin Hoffert,
New York University

"Proved reserves of oil, gas and coal remain more than adequate to meet the world's growing needs (in aggregate) for the foreseeable future."

Peter Davies, BP Chief Economist

Sun, wind and water

The three most familiar sources of renewable energy are the Sun, wind and water. Sunlight can be used to heat water and to generate electricity. The wind's energy can be harnessed to turn turbines that generate electricity. The wind blows across the sea, producing huge waves. Wave machines can capture the energy from these waves. Energy can also be harnessed to produce electricity from the power of moving water in rivers and from the movement of the tides. Heat energy from rocks inside the Earth can be used to heat water and generate electricity.

Straight from the Sun

The Sun is a huge energy source. At its centre, nuclear reactions called 'nuclear fusion' are releasing enormous amounts of energy as heat and light. The Sun could meet all of our energy needs many times over, if only we could harness its energy effectively. Since the Sun will be shining for many millions of years to come, solar energy is sustainable.

Almost all our energy comes from the Sun. Without this energy, in the form of heat and light, life on Earth would be impossible.

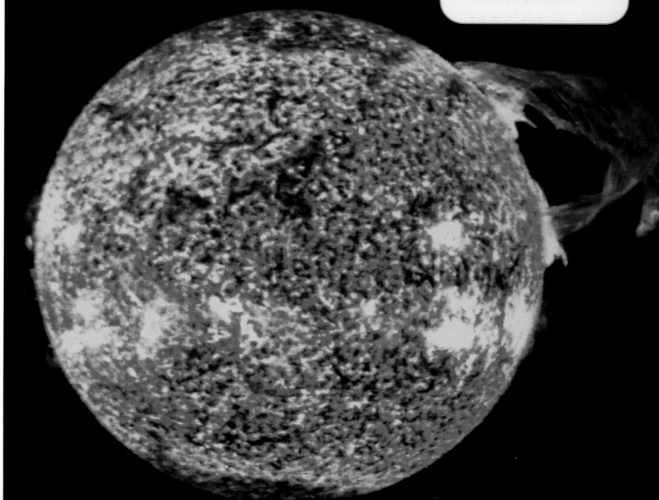

In sunny climates a solar panel on the roof of a house can supply enough hot water for the entire family.

Earth's powerhouse

The remains of plants that absorbed the Sun's energy millions of years ago are used in fossil fuels. The Sun's energy drives the wind and waves. The Sun powers the water cycle, too. This causes rainfall and the running water used for hydroelectric power. The Sun's energy is used by plants to produce food and fuels such as wood. Animals get their energy by eating plants or by eating other animals that have eaten plants.

Solar energy to heat water

One of the ways in which we can harness the energy of the Sun directly is by using it to heat water. Today, there are many different systems and techniques – from those that heat swimming pools to advanced systems that can heat water to over 150°C for industrial purposes. The most common are solar panels or solar collectors. Water circulating through the solar panel is heated and stored in a large tank. Solar panels on roofs can provide hot water for heating houses and for showers and baths. There are probably as many as 5 million domestic solar systems in use around the world. Once installed, solar systems provide free hot water with no damaging effects to the environment.

Solar energy facts

▶ The first solar hot water heating system was developed in the USA in the early 1900s.

▶ The first solar collector was a wooden box with a glass top and black base. John Herschel cooked his food in it on an expedition to Africa. He recorded a temperature of nearly 90°C.

The air in a conservatory built on the southern side of a building heats up quickly. This warm air can be circulated to other rooms.

Passive solar heating

Passive solar heating makes use of the sunlight that floods into rooms on sunny days. Once inside the room, the heat is trapped by the glass in the window. This is a free source of heat. Even on dull and cloudy days, a south-facing room can be quite warm. The shape of a building and the materials from which it is made will affect the amount of sunlight that reaches inside the rooms. With carefully positioned windows and skylights, a building can be warmed. This is known as passive solar design. A glass conservatory traps heat, too. By using the right materials, a whole building becomes a heat store – warming up in the day and releasing the heat when it is needed. Passive solar designs have cut energy costs in some US homes by up to 40 per cent.

Photovoltaics

In 1839, the French scientist Henri Becquerel discovered that light falling on certain materials produced electricity. He called this the 'photovoltaic effect' ('photo' for light and 'voltaic' for electricity). Now there are photovoltaic panels that convert light energy directly into electricity. A photovoltaic cell contains thin layers of silicon. When light strikes the cell electrons move between the layers of silicon and this produces an electrical current. The more light there is, the greater the amount of electricity produced. The first photovoltaic cells were very expensive to make and only a fraction of the light that fell on them was converted into electricity. However, the latest cells are far more efficient and much cheaper to make.

Photovoltaic cells were originally developed for use in space to power satellites. Now they are used around the world. The electricity can be used to power household or office equipment, to charge batteries for telephones or laptops or to run garden lights or fountains. Photovoltaic cells require minimal maintenance and the running costs are tiny, so they are ideal for use in remote places of the world. In isolated parts of the world, photovoltaic panels can be used to run water pumps for drinking water and for powering refrigerators to store food and medicines.

Solar power stations

Solar energy can also be used to drive power stations. Solar One is a solar power station in California, USA, that produces electricity by focusing the Sun's heat on a steam-powered electricity generator using 1800 mirrors. The mirrors follow the Sun as it moves across the sky making sure that the sunlight is always directed onto the generator. This massive system in southern California produces 99 per cent of the USA's solar-generated electricity and supplies energy to the homes of hundreds of thousands of people. There are other designs of solar power stations. Some have a series of trough-shaped mirrors that reflect the light onto steel pipes at the bottom, heating the liquid inside to a staggering 400°C.

This array of trough-shaped mirrors in the Mojave Desert, California, uses the Sun's energy to generate electricity.

Wind energy

Wind is a truly sustainable source of energy as it is renewable and does not create any harmful emissions or wastes. Currently, the amount of electricity generated worldwide by wind energy is the equivalent of twenty typical coal-fired power stations and this is increasing each year. Most wind farms are built on land but there are some wind farms out at sea. In addition, there are millions of small wind turbines around the world that are used to pump water. Although they do not generate electricity they avoid the need to use electricity to pump the water.

How a turbine works

Modern wind turbines are efficient, reliable and long lasting. They may run for up to 6000 hours a year for as long as 25 years. They can generate from 50 watts to 2000 kilowatts of electricity. The ideal wind speed for electricity generation is from 6 to 25 metres per second. Then, the steel blades turn 34 times a minute – the best speed for maximum efficiency. A wind vane feeds information about the wind speed and direction to the turbine's computer, controlling the speed of the blades. The speed of the turbines is controlled by a yaw motor, which turns the blades to face the wind. In storm conditions the computer puts the blades in a stop position and the generator is switched off.

Despite objections about the way wind farms look and the noise they create, research has shown that many people feel the advantages of wind farms make up for any disadvantages. In Scotland, for example, 90 per cent of tourists said that nearby wind farms made no difference to the enjoyment of their holiday. In fact, in some cases, wind farms can themselves be tourist attractions! However, residents who live very close to the wind farms experience noise and flickering light as the rotating blades reflect the sunlight.

Small wind turbines can be built to supply electricity to remote farms and communities.

Wind energy facts

▶ In the year 2000 alone, 3800 megawatts of new wind energy generating capacity was installed around the world.

▶ In Denmark wind turbines produce 17 per cent of the country's electricity.

▶ Using a 1-megawatt wind turbine to generate electricity will cut more than 2000 tons of carbon dioxide emissions every year.

Out to sea

It is possible to put wind farms out to sea. Offshore wind turbines tend to be larger than land turbines and wind speed is higher. Some of the largest offshore turbines are between 60 and 80 metres tall with 30-metre-long blades. Offshore wind technology is still quite new. The first offshore wind farm was built off the coast of Denmark in 1991 and the second was built in 1996. Sweden, the Netherlands and the UK now have their own wind farms. It costs twice as much to build wind farms at sea than on land. But the cost of building an offshore wind farm is covered by the sale of the electricity produced within seven to ten years. There are usually fewer objections to offshore wind farms from the public, but there are considerable environmental concerns regarding disturbance and pollution of valuable wildlife habitats, especially during the construction phase.

"This is a great opportunity for people to co-own a wind farm and do their bit in the fight against climate change and dwindling energy supplies."

Steve Lunn, a director of Westmill Wind Co-op in Oxfordshire, UK, on building a wind farm owned by local residents

"This news will remove from hundreds of local inhabitants the threat that has been hanging over them for the last two years and enable them to get on with their lives."

Dorset Against Rural Turbines (Dart) spokesperson, on hearing that a scheme to build nine controversial 104-metre wind turbines in Dorset, UK, had been scrapped

In the sea near Copenhagen in Denmark, wind turbines harness wind energy. Although more expensive to build than wind farms on land, offshore wind farms are placed away from people and do not take up valuable land.

Hydropower

Moving water has been used for centuries to drive water wheels for machinery and for milling corn. Water wheels can also be used to generate electricity. The name usually used for turning water energy into electricity is hydroelectric power or hydropower. Hydroelectric schemes are used in many countries around the world. They are common in countries with mountains and high rainfall where water streaming down to the sea can be dammed and used to turn turbines.

At present, hydropower provides about 10 per cent of the world's electricity but this figure will increase when the Three Gorges Dam in China is in use (see page 9). Currently, the largest hydroelectric dam in the world is the Itaipu Dam in Brazil. It can generate the same amount of electricity as twelve nuclear power stations.

Hydro facts

▸ There are 80,000 dams across rivers in the USA but only 2400 are currently used for hydroelectricity.

▸ Worldwide, hydroelectric plants can generate up to 675,000 megawatts of electricity – the energy equivalent to 3.6 billion barrels of oil!

▸ Currently the largest dam in the world, Itaipu Dam in Brazil, produces 13,320 megawatts of electricity but will be upgraded to roughly 20,000 megawatts.

▸ The largest dam in the USA is the Grand Coulee Dam in Washington State. It produces 7600 megawatts and there are plans to increase this to 10,800 megawatts.

Huge turbines are located deep inside a dam. Falling water spins the turbines and this drives the generators.

How does a turbine work?

Moving water strikes a turbine and makes it rotate. This drives a generator to make electricity. The amount of electricity that can be generated at any site depends on how fast the water is flowing and how strongly it pushes on the turbine. The further the water falls to reach the turbine, the higher the pressure. Large schemes use a dam and a reservoir. The reservoir stores the water until it is needed. Smaller scale schemes built in rivers make use of the moving water to generate smaller amounts of electricity.

The construction of the Glen Canyon Dam on the Colorado River in Arizona, USA, was completed in 1963 and since then it has supplied electricity to much of south-west USA.

Case Study: The Snowy Mountains hydroelectric scheme, Australia

The Snowy Mountains hydroelectric scheme is the biggest engineering project ever undertaken in Australia. This hydroelectric scheme, built in a national park, is one of the most complex, multi-purpose, multi-reservoir hydro schemes in the world. It took 25 years to build and consists of sixteen major dams, seven power stations, a pumping station, and 225 kilometres of inter-connected tunnels, pipelines and aqueducts. The scheme has had a huge environmental impact, but careful planning has ensured that damage has been minimal. It generates clean, sustainable energy to eastern mainland Australia, while operating responsibly within the unique environment of the Snowy Mountains.

Wave energy

Waves are created by the wind blowing across the surface of the sea. The distance the wind blows across the water is called its 'fetch'. The greater the fetch of the wind, the stronger the waves. At the surface, waves rise and fall, spilling over onto the shore as breakers. This up and down motion can be converted into electricity.

> The wave energy converter known as the Mighty Whale can extract energy from waves and convert it into electricity or heat energy.

Case Study: The Mighty Whale

Off the coast of Japan, near the mouth of Gokasho Bay, there is a wave device called the Mighty Whale. The waves press on air inside the device and this in turn moves air turbines. The turbines drive the generators. Because it absorbs and converts the energy of the waves, the Mighty Whale creates a calm sea space behind it that can be used for water sports or fish farming.

Harnessing wave power

There are four ways to harness the power of the waves:

- One kind of wave energy device is like a giant bicycle pump. You pump up the tyres of a bicycle by pushing a piston through a tube. The piston forces the air into the bicycle tyre. With this wave device, as the water crashes onto the coast it pushes the column of air through a turbine. The Hebrides is a group of islands to the north of Scotland, and on Islay, one of the Inner Hebrides, there is a simple and effective wave device that makes use of wave power in this way to generate electricity for homes and for charging electric buses.

- A second way of using wave power is with undersea turbines similar to those used in ordinary power stations. Water flows through the device and turns turbines to generate electricity.

- 'Salter's duck' is the name given to a device that uses cam-shapes, which rotate around an axle, or spine, as the waves pass, generating power. The original Salter's duck was invented in the 1970s by Stephen Salter and it has undergone continual development since. The duck is a moving float, secured by a line to the seabed. The latest 'duck' consists of dozens of pistons fixed inside a cylinder. The pistons are pushed in and out as the duck bobs up and down on the water and this generates electricity.

- Finally, a raft converter uses a raft with hinged sections. As waves pass underneath the hinged sections, power is generated.

Case Study: Pelamis

Pelamis is a raft converter being trialled off the coast of Scotland. It is like four railway carriages with flexible connections, so each 'carriage' rises and falls with the waves like a train going over hills. The energy from the movement of the raft converter can be harnessed using power conversion modules. The full-scale prototype contains three power conversion modules, each producing 250 kilowatts of electricity. It was tested at sea on 1 April 2004 and successfully generated electricity from the waves. Since then, Pelamis has provided sustainable electricity to 500 homes.

The Pelamis wave energy converter being tested.

Waterfowl such as these Canada Geese rely on estuary habitats for their survival. Although tidal barrages provide renewable energy, they can be harmful to natural habitats and endanger wildlife.

Tidal energy

The tides move a huge amount of water each day and it is possible to harness the energy from tides to generate electricity. Although this source of energy is reliable and renewable, harnessing it is expensive. In order to use tidal energy there needs to be a large tidal range – a large difference in the high tide compared with the low tide. The average rise and fall of the tides along a coast is around 1 metre but for schemes to be successful there needs to be a rise and fall of at least 5 metres. However, there is a much larger tidal range in river estuaries. There are only about twenty sites in the world that are suitable for harnessing tidal energy, of which eight are around the coast of the UK.

Tidal barrages

A tidal barrage is a large dam built across an estuary with a series of turbines at the bottom. The turbines turn as the water flows through. Some barrages generate electricity from the force of an incoming tide. Others trap the water behind a barrage, which then opens up to generate electricity as the tide goes out. Sometimes the currents of both the incoming and outgoing tides are used. The tidal barrage with the largest tidal range is the Bay of Fundy in Canada. Its range is 16 metres and the barrage supplies enough electricity for 4000 homes.

Tidal devices are sustainable – the energy is free and no waste is produced (once the barrage is constructed), and they are also cheap to maintain. However, they have considerable impact on the ecology of an estuary. Tidal barrages and dams flood marshlands and wetlands – traditionally the habitats in which migrating birds feed and recover from their flights. In addition, by blocking a river, a tidal barrage or dam can prevent spawning fish travelling upstream.

Case Study: La Rance estuary

The tides in La Rance estuary in France are among the highest in the world. Turbines under its power station are turned by the changing tides, which spin generators that produce the electricity. Gates are used to trap the tides so that electricity can be produced when it is needed. The power station could act as a huge barrier to fish and other living things in the river. However, careful planning allows wildlife to move freely past it, so the power station is environmentally friendly. The tidal scheme on the Rance estuary has been generating approximately 480 gigawatt hours of electricity a year ever since it was finished in 1967, enough to power about 200,000 homes. Similar tidal schemes have been built in Canada and China. Tidal schemes are expensive to build, but putting a road or rail link across the barrage can give the scheme more than one use.

This barrage on the River Rance in France has been generating electricity from the tides since 1967. There is an 8-metre tidal range and electricity is generated on the rise and fall of the tide.

Hot water from the Earth

Scientists believe that Earth was formed from a huge, swirling mass of dust about 4700 million years ago. As the dust particles collided, they took the temperature of the new planet (Earth) to around 1000°C. The surface cooled, but the centre, or core, stayed hot. Earth's core is around 3000°C and is a huge store of heat energy.

In the volcanic areas of the world such as Iceland, New Zealand and parts of North America, the hot rocks lie close to the surface. The rocks heat up water that lies deep in the ground. This extremely hot water forces its way upward towards the surface through cracks in the rock. Most of this water remains underground but a hot spring is formed where the hot water escapes to the surface.

Geothermal energy

Geothermal power uses heat energy from inside the Earth. The easiest way to use this energy is to pump out the Earth's naturally hot water and use it to heat buildings or to produce steam for generating electricity. Another way to harness this heat is to drill two holes into hot dry rock. This method is known as HDR. Cold water is pumped down one hole and seeps through cracks in the hot rocks and is heated up. This hot water is then pumped up to the surface through the other hole. This method is still to be used commercially.

Hot water at this Icelandic geothermal power station is used to generate electricity. The waste water from the power station is still warm and is used to heat the Blue Lagoon, a popular recreational pool.

Geothermal power stations generate electricity using the Earth's natural heat. This geothermal power station in New Zealand makes use of the volcanic nature of the country's geology.

The plentiful supply of geothermal energy has allowed Iceland to become Europe's largest producer of bananas. These fruits naturally grow on tropical plants in the hottest countries of the world, but they can also be grown in cold countries in heated greenhouses. Italy, France, Germany, Japan, New Zealand and the USA all use some geothermal energy.

Environmental issues

Geothermal energy is a clean source of energy but there are some environmental concerns regarding the recycling of the water once it has been used. Some of the latest geothermal projects inject used water back into the ground to replace the hot water that has been pumped out. However, care has to be taken that this water does not cool down nearby hot springs.

Case Study: Rotokawa, New Zealand

The Rotokawa power station in New Zealand taps natural underground steam and hot water to generate electricity. It works in combination with a hydroelectric scheme, contributing about 10 per cent of the electricity produced. The power station has less environmental impact than a coal-burning power station, and farming and forestry take place all around it. Geothermal schemes do produce some carbon dioxide, but far less than a fossil fuel power station of similar size.

Energy from waste

How much waste do you throw away every week? Every year, the UK alone produces 428 million tons of waste. This includes 30 million tons of domestic waste, 50 million tons of industrial waste and 119 million tons of mineral extraction waste. Most of the domestic, industrial and building waste is buried in landfill sites, where it decays. One way this refuse could be reused is to produce energy in a refuse-burning power station. Recycling is another way of reusing the waste while in some parts of the world waste is used to produce a gas that can be used as a fuel.

Electricity from waste

Refuse-derived fuel, or RDF, is made by sorting and shredding rubbish that can be made into pellets. Power stations burn these pellets of waste to heat water to produce steam. The steam drives a turbine that generates electricity. At present, there are only four RDF plants in the UK. One of these – the Byker RDF plant in Newcastle-upon-Tyne – supplies enough energy to heat 200 homes. Also there are many waste-to-energy incinerators where waste is burnt and the heat used to produce steam for electricity generation.

Protection from pollution

Burning solid waste sounds like a great idea, but there are problems. Burning refuse produces carbon dioxide as well as toxic gases. The chimneys have to be carefully designed to remove unpleasant or even dangerous emissions. Devices called scrubbers clean the gases before they reach the atmosphere. The ash produced by burning RDF has to be buried in a landfill site.

Huge mountains of waste are common in some large cities. Here in Manila, the capital of the Philippines, the waste is being spread out before being sorted by people who will sell useful items such as metal and plastic. This way the amount of waste is reduced.

In Finland and Switzerland more than 90 per cent of glass is recycled. In the UK only about 34 per cent is recycled and the rest ends up in landfills. Each ton of cullet used saves on 1.2 tons of raw materials.

Biogas

Much of our waste is buried in landfill sites where it decays naturally. A product of this decay is biogas, a flammable gas that is rich in methane. Every tonne of waste produces 100 times its own volume of gas. Biogas has a high energy content. When biogas is burnt, far less carbon dioxide is released than when fossil fuels are burnt. Worldwide, there are over 140 schemes that tap into the gas from underground rubbish. In the UK, 50 of the 400 landfill sites around the country tap biogas and use it to generate electricity. This saves 250,000 tons of coal every year. However, most landfill sites just allow the gas to escape into the atmosphere, where the methane contributes to global warming.

In 2005, Sweden unveiled an environmentally friendly biogas-powered passenger train – said to be the world's first. The train, fitted with two biogas bus engines, can carry up to 54 passengers, and will run on Sweden's east coast between Linkoeping and Vaestervik. The train can run for 600 kilometres before it needs to refuel and can reach a speed of 130 kilometres per hour. Sweden already has 779 biogas buses and thousands of cars running on a mixture of petrol and biogas.

Recycling

The amount of waste produced can be reduced by manufacturers cutting down on the amount of packaging they use and by households recycling more waste. Recycling reduces the demand for raw materials. Often it takes less energy to make something from recycled materials than from raw materials. For example, making a new aluminium can from recycled aluminium saves enough energy to power a light bulb for six hours.

Glass is for ever

Glass never wears out – it can be endlessly recycled. Glass is made from three materials: sand, soda ash and limestone. These materials are put in a furnace and heated to about 1500°C until they melt. The heat needed to make glass is usually produced by burning fossil fuels. When recycled glass is used, it is sorted, cleaned and crushed to form cullet. Cullet melts at a lower temperature than the raw materials, so far less fuel is needed when recycled glass is used, and less carbon dioxide is released. When glass is recycled, less waste ends up in landfills.

Biofuels

Unlike fossil fuels, which come from the fossilized remains of living matter, biofuels come from plants that are grown for fuel or from plant wastes. They come from many different sources, including wood, straw and energy crops such as sugar cane. Biofuels can be used to produce heat energy, electricity and fuel. We will not run out of the plants used to make biofuels, so they are a renewable source of energy.

Energy from plants

Wood and other parts of plants have been used as a fuel by humans for millions of years to keep warm and to cook. Wood is still the primary source of energy in many developing countries. Biofuels are derived from many sorts of plant matter including young trees that are cut down or 'thinned' to make room for others, wooden pallets, construction waste, and lawn trimmings.

When wood is burnt its stored chemical energy is converted into other forms of energy such as heat or electricity. This process is carbon neutral, which means that it does not result in an increase of carbon dioxide in the Earth's atmosphere. This is because when biofuels are burnt the same amount of carbon dioxide is released as the plants absorbed when they were growing. Burning biofuels produces some waste gases such as sulphur dioxide, but in far smaller quantities than those emitted by coal-burning power stations.

In many countries, including Kenya, wood is still a major energy source, and people walk many miles each day to find and collect wood for burning on stoves.

Ethanol-powered cars

In the mid 1980s – before any other country even thought of the idea – Brazil succeeded in mass-producing a biofuel for motor vehicles: ethanol (a type of alcohol), derived from its plentiful supplies of sugar cane. Ethanol can also be produced from sugar-rich crops such as sugar beet and maize. The sugar is extracted from the plant and allowed to ferment, producing ethanol.

Ethanol is used widely in Brazil where it is mixed with petrol to form gasohol. Gasohol is 80 to 90 per cent petrol and 10 to 20 per cent ethanol. Gasohol burns cleaner and more efficiently than normal petrol so this has helped to reduce air pollution in some of Brazil's traffic-clogged cities. Gasohol-powered cars tend to have smaller engines than conventional cars. This reduces the weight of the cars so less energy is required to move them.

Ethanol and petrol mixes are used widely in the USA, especially in cities that suffer from air pollution such as Los Angeles. The petrol mix contains about 6 per cent ethanol by volume. The presence of just a small amount of ethanol makes the fuel burn more cleanly.

Biodiesel

Biodiesel is a fuel that could one day replace petroleum-based diesel as the main fuel for vehicles. It is a fuel made from renewable resources such as vegetable oils or animal fats. It is biodegradable (breaks down in the environment) and non-toxic, and it produces fewer emissions than petroleum-based diesel when burnt. It can even be used in diesel engines without any modifications to the engines.

The main sources of the vegetable oils are oil-seed rape, soybeans, oil palms and coconuts. The seeds of these plants are full of oil that can be extracted. One hectare of oil-seed rape yields about 3 tons of seeds. The seeds produce about 1500 litres of oil that can be made into fuel and 1.6 tons of high-protein seedcake that can be used to feed livestock. The seedcake can also be fermented to make ethanol, as can the stalks and leaves of the crop. Soybeans yield about 900 litres per hectare. The yields from coconuts and oil palms are much greater (3000 and 7500 litres respectively) but these plants take much longer to grow. Coconuts and oil palms are widely grown in tropical regions of the world and could provide developing countries with a sustainable source of fuel and lessen their dependency on the oil-producing countries.

The petrol sold in this Brazilian service station is made from a petrol-ethanol mix to reduce the amount of pollutants produced by the car engine.

Energy from straw

Once crops have been harvested, the stubble and plant remains may be left to decay, or simply burnt to clear the ground. Modern techniques can use this waste to generate energy. Straw stubble can be burnt to heat water, and then the steam produced turns the blades of a turbine, generating electricity. Wood waste can be used in the same way.

Case Study: Free fuel in Slovakia

The first straw-burning facility in Slovakia was built at a farm in Prasice close to Bratislava. The facility is on a large agricultural farm with 50 square kilometres of arable (crop) land. They produce wheat and keep 1000 cattle. Until 1993, the straw left after the harvest stayed on the land to rot. Then a straw burner was imported from the UK, and the heat produced from burning the straw was used to supply hot water for central heating in the offices, farm buildings and apartments on the site. The straw is dry and produces little smoke when it is burnt, and the ash is used as fertiliser. The savings were enormous – in three years the boiler had paid for itself.

Ely Power Station in the UK is the largest straw-burning power station in the world, generating 270 gigawatt hours of electricity each year. It burns 200,000 tons of straw each year, which is supplied by local farmers.

Some fast-growing species of trees such as willow and poplar can be planted as a crop. Every few years the trees are harvested, leaving a stump that regrows. This is a sustainable source of wood.

Coppicing

Coppicing is an efficient way of getting energy from plants. Trees such as willow or poplar, or tropical grasses such as Miscanthus are grown quickly and regularly cropped. Their growing tops are cut, leaving the roots. In developing countries, the cuttings are burnt in stoves. In developed countries, the crop is dried and chipped and burnt in power stations. The roots remain and the trees grow again. Every few years, they can be cropped again. Biofuels from tree cuttings produce ten times the energy that is used to plant, grow and harvest the trees.

Biodigestors

In some parts of Asia and Africa, large underground chambers called biodigestors are used to produce cooking gas from cow dung.

The dung is put in a tank where it rots, producing biogas. The biogas can be piped to a gas ring and used for cooking and heating. The rotted cow dung can then be used as fertiliser.

In the rural areas of many parts of India there is no electricity supply as the areas are too far away from the nearest power station. In order to improve the standard of living of people in these rural communities the government is providing biodigesters which supply enough biogas for cooking and heating and to fuel small electricity generators. This will make these communities self sufficient in electricity.

Being energy efficient

We could reduce our impact on the environment, and save money as well, if we all used less energy. This means thinking about our use of energy-consuming heating, lighting and transport. It also means taking care that we use the least energy in every situation. Walking to school, cycling to work and putting on warm clothes rather than turning up the heating all save energy. By using less energy we need less fuel and we produce less waste.

Insulating your home

One way to reduce the amount of energy needed to heat a home is to make sure the building is well insulated. Insulation slows down the rate at which heat escapes. It is a bit like wearing a padded jacket in winter to keep the body warm. A hot water boiler surrounded by insulation will lose heat more slowly than one without. Many good insulators are thick, loose-woven materials. Because of the loose weave, they trap air in their fibres, and air is a good insulator that retains heat.

This thermogram of a house shows the temperature of all the surfaces. The temperature range goes from hot (white and yellow) to cold (blue). The windows are yellow and white, indicating that heat is being lost. Less heat is escaping through the roof.

Case Study: Environmentally friendly buildings at Butzbach, Germany

In Butzbach, Germany, there is a technical college that trains young engineers to design environmentally friendly buildings. The college building itself was created as an example of this. Its large windows face south so they collect the maximum amount of the Sun's heat. Different insulation materials are used in different parts of the building so that students can compare how well they work. A large mirror near the building reflects sunlight onto four smaller mirrors, which in turn reflect the light into the building. The reflected light can save electricity because there is no need to switch all the lights on. One of the mirrors also reflects sunlight onto an internal wall made of heat-storing sandstone. This releases heat slowly, keeping the rooms warm.

These buildings in Santorini, Greece, are designed to keep cool in the hot summer. The white walls reflect away the sunlight while the windows are small so the rooms stay cool. This reduces the need to use air conditioning units that use a lot of energy.

Loft insulation and double glazing

In cold countries, more than 50 per cent of the energy used in a house is for heating. Heat rises, and 25 per cent of this energy can escape through the roof if it is not properly insulated. A thick blanket in the loft or attic of a house helps to retain heat. With loft insulation such as this, instead of warming the air above the roof, the heat will be warming the rooms below it.

Some energy also escapes through windows. A single sheet of glass is a poor insulator and lets the heat through easily. Two sheets of glass can sandwich the air between them. This is called double glazing, and it works because air is a good insulator. It slows the speed that heat travels. Some double glazing panels have a vacuum, where there is nothing – not even air – between the glass sheets. This vacuum is even better than air at retaining heat.

Paying for itself

Good insulation eventually pays for itself because of saving on fuel costs. Loft insulation, for example, will pay for itself over about two years. Double glazing is not so effective, but it will still pay for itself over twenty years. Simple changes such as wrapping a hot water tank in insulation make a real difference. Even draught-proofing exterior doors and windows will save energy. Governments and local authorities often support energy-saving improvements on homes with grants and tax breaks.

These energy-efficient homes in Denmark are made from recycled materials. They have natural turf roofs to help retain heat. The electricity comes from a small wind turbine built nearby.

Energy-efficient homes

A modern house uses a lot of energy. Fuel is needed for the central heating system, which keeps the house warm and provides hot water, and electricity is needed for lighting. Now it is possible to build houses that are energy efficient. In fact some are so efficient that they do not need a central heating system. This is achieved by using new materials, plenty of insulation and heat exchange systems. Some of the latest designs of heat exchangers make use of the waste hot water from showers that goes down the drain. The pipes carrying the hot waste water away are used to heat cold water going into the boiler, so saving on the amount of energy that is required to heat the water.

In Yealmpton, a village in Devon, England, an example of an energy-efficient house has been built. This house is insulated like a huge storage heater made of concrete blocks. It uses solar heating, a heat exchange system and natural air circulation to save on fuel costs. Efficient insulation means the house will stay at the same core temperature all year round. There is a system to collect rainwater and use it to flush toilets and to run the washing machine. Mains water is used only for drinking, cooking and showering and electricity is provided by solar panels on the roof. Although the house cost 20 per cent more to build than a conventional house because of the unusual building techniques, money will be saved on heating and electricity costs. The house may even be able to sell its excess electricity to the national electricity system.

Controlling energy use

All central heating systems have a thermostat – a device that turns the boiler down or off when your home reaches a target temperature. Timers can switch on the central heating when you most need it, for example, early on a cold morning. But computer control makes it far easier to manage our use of energy. It controls the temperature and the timing of heating much more precisely, reducing waste and improving energy efficiency.

Case Study: Santa Monica's Sustainable City Program

Since 1994, when it established the Sustainable City Program, Santa Monica, on the Pacific coast of California in the USA, has been a leader in the construction of environmentally friendly buildings and the use of renewable energy and waste diversion. In 2005 the city negotiated with an electricity provider to provide 100 per cent of the city's buildings with electricity generated from renewable sources.

The electricity will come from a geothermal power station, wind turbines and solar power installations. In addition, 67 per cent of the city's solid waste is either recycled or reused in some way, a figure that is much higher than most other US cities. The city is now trying to improve air quality by reducing the number of cars driven around the city.

Santa Monica, California, is an environmentally friendly city, but that doesn't stop the lights shining. Santa Monica is aiming to be the world's first energy-efficient city. It offers encouragement to residents in homes and businesses who want to become energy efficient.

Going places

There are around 400 million cars currently in use around the world. Europe and the USA have much higher levels of car ownership than other countries. In China, there are only about eight vehicles per 1000 persons, and in India, only seven per 1000 persons; by contrast, there are about 750 motor vehicles per 1000 persons in the USA. Worldwide, traffic has grown by more than 50 per cent in the past ten years. In the UK, nearly 200,000 tons of carbon dioxide is emitted each year just by cars carrying 11- to 15-year-olds to school. More energy-efficient transport is desperately needed and car manufacturers are working to find cleaner, more efficient fuels.

Most cars run on petrol or diesel fuel that, when burnt, emits greenhouse gases such as carbon dioxide as well as some unburned hydrocarbons. These greenhouse gases contribute to acid rain and climate change. The average car will last for ten to twelve years, may cover 320,000 kilometres in that time, consume 4.5 litres of fuel every 64 kilometres and need an oil change every 32,000 kilometres using around 4.5 litres of motor oil each time. These figures are based on a medium-sized 1.6 petrol model – some cars will consume a great deal more than this.

Traditionally, most people in China have travelled around their cities by bicycle as they could not afford to buy a car. This is changing as standards of living improve. Now the government is having to tackle the problems of traffic congestion and pollution.

This is one of an increasing number of energy-efficient hybrid cars. This car combines a conventional car engine and an electric motor. The petrol motor is for speed on major roads and the electric motor is for efficiency around towns.

Dual fuel or hybrid cars

A new type of hybrid car combines a petrol engine with an electric motor. For each litre of fuel it uses, a hybrid car can travel 8–12 kilometres further than a standard car. The electric motor can work on its own when the car is being driven at lower speeds, such as those used around towns. Once the vehicle reaches higher speeds, the petrol engine takes over. Under hard acceleration, both the petrol engine and the electric motor can work together to provide the power.

The hybrid car has a battery that provides the energy for the electric motor. This battery is recharged by capturing energy that would normally be lost when the driver brakes and the car slows down. This is called regenerative braking. If needed, power from the petrol engine can be diverted to recharge the battery as well. This means that hybrid cars never need to be plugged in.

Smooth shapes and lightweight materials

Fuel use can be reduced in other ways, too. Cars with a streamlined shape are more efficient. A streamlined shape makes air flow around a car more easily, reducing air friction. This means less energy is needed to drive the car forward. Modern cars weigh less thanks to the increased use of materials such as aluminium and plastic. A car that weighs less travels more miles on a litre of petrol than a similar size of car that weighs more.

What you can do

We can make a difference by thinking about how we use energy in every aspect of our lives – at school, at home and in the places where we go to relax and enjoy ourselves. If we do all this, wherever we live, we can ensure energy use will be more sustainable in the future.

Saving energy

You can save energy by reducing the amount you use and by more efficient use of the energy you need. Only turning on the heating when you are really cold and wearing extra clothes instead of turning the heating up will save fuel. Not wasting heat by leaving the windows and doors open on cold days will make even more savings. You can also make big savings by turning off lights you do not need. Low-energy bulbs use far less energy than conventional bulbs. Turning televisions, stereos and computers off at night, rather than leaving them on standby, will save both energy and money.

Showers use less water than baths so they use less energy because there is less water to heat. Only putting as much water in the kettle as you need saves both water and the energy used to heat it. Glass, paper, metal and plastic can all be recycled rather than thrown in the bin.

People often jump in the car to drive very short distances. This wastes energy, clogs up the roads and produces a lot of pollution. You can save energy by walking or cycling to school or going by public transport.

By recycling glass, plastic, metal and paper you can help reduce the demand for energy. It often takes less energy to make something from recycled materials than from raw materials.

Working together

You could start a campaign, working with others to get your community or school to review their use of energy. Many schools are finding ways of saving energy by fitting low-energy light bulbs, insulating buildings and by buying energy-efficient machines. This could result in huge savings – and that money could be spent on more teachers in a school, more books and computers, better facilities at leisure centres, and more pleasant surroundings. Students at one school monitored their school's energy use. They found that the caretaker turned every light on in the school at night, and only turned each room's light off after he had finished cleaning the room. A huge saving was made when the caretaker only kept each room's light on while he was working in it.

Saving the world

All of us are greenhouse gas producers. When we make a journey, buy a product or switch on a light we are usually contributing, although indirectly, to global warming. Each of us can make a contribution to sustainability. Simple acts, such as walking or cycling rather than making a short journey by car, turning off lights and not leaving devices on standby, all help to reduce fuel bills and carbon dioxide emissions. With care, we can all make our footprint on the Earth as small as possible and ensure that we preserve the world's precious resources for future generations.

Glossary

acid rain rain made acidic by polluting gases in the atmosphere such as sulphur dioxide. Acid rain harms trees and damages ancient buildings.

biodiesel fuel made from renewable resources such as vegetable oils or animal fats

biofuel fuel derived immediately from living matter

biogas mix of gases produced by rotting organic matter. Biogas can be used as a fuel.

crude oil oil in its natural state, when it has first been extracted and not yet processed or refined

developed country wealthy country that is technologically advanced

developing country financially poor and technologically unsophisticated country that is becoming more advanced

emission substance, such as gas, given off or discharged. Carbon dioxide, for example, is an emission produced by burning fossil fuels such as coal.

estuary place where a river meets the sea

ferment undergo chemical breakdown by bacteria, yeasts or other micro-organisms

fossil fuel substance such as coal, oil or natural gas that is formed from the decayed remains of plants and animals.

geothermal relating to or produced by the heat from inside Earth. Geothermal power stations harness this heat to produce energy.

global warming gradual rise in the overall temperature of Earth's surface caused by an increase in the concentration of greenhouse gases in the atmosphere

habitat place where a plant or animal lives

hybrid car car that combines a petrol engine with an electric motor to save fuel

hydrocarbon substance or compound made up of hydrogen and carbon. Hydrocarbons are found in oil and natural gas.

hydroelectric power electricity generated by the movement of water

insulator substance that slows down the movement of heat, sound or electricity. Good insulation can slow down the loss of heat from your home and so help to save energy.

landfill site place where waste material or refuse is gathered together and buried

molecule group of atoms joined together

non-renewable fuels fuels, such as fossil fuels, that come from any source that does not renew itself quickly and so will eventually be used up

nuclear power energy generated by controlled nuclear fission (the splitting of an atomic nucleus) inside the core of a nuclear reactor

oil refinery chemical plant where crude oil is separated into useful 'fractions', including fuel oils and lubricating oils

photosynthesis process by which green plants use sunlight to make nutrients, or food, from carbon dioxide and water

pollution presence of high levels of harmful substances in the environment, often as a result of human activity

radioactivity release of radiation (a type of electromagnetic energy) from the atomic nuclei of radioactive substances

renewable resources sources of energy, such as the Sun, wind, water or geothermal energy, that are replenished and will not run out

soil erosion wearing away of soil and land by rain, rivers or wind

solar panel sheet that absorbs the Sun's rays as an energy source

sustainable able to continue to support itself indefinitely. A sustainable environment is in balance, so that natural resources are not wasted.

tidal barrage dam across a river estuary that uses tidal movement to generate electricity

turbine wheel-shaped machine for producing power. The wheel is usually fitted with blades or cups to catch moving water, steam, gas or air in order to turn the wheel and produce power.

Further information

Websites

WWF International

www.panda.org

WWF US

www.worldwildlife.org

WWF-UK

www.wwf.org.uk

WWF is an international charity that takes action to protect species and tackle threats to the environment for the benefit of people and nature. It works for sustainable development.

www.foe.co.uk

This Friends of the Earth website includes lots of information on the use of sustainable energy and tips on how to save energy.

www.wri.org

This website of the World Resources Institute covers all the main issues regarding the debate surrounding energy and global warming.

www.iaeel.org

The International Association for Energy Efficient Lighting provides useful information and tips on low-energy light bulbs.

www.natenergy.org.uk

The website of the National Energy Foundation covers everything you need to know about renewable energy including a list of Energy Efficiency Advice Centres in the UK.

www.greenpeace.org

Greenpeace is an international organisation that focuses on worldwide threats to the environment, including global warming and climate change.

www.create.org.uk

Create is an organisation that aims to educate people in ways to achieve more sustainable uses of energy and reduce carbon emissions.

Books

Essential Energy: Energy Alternatives, Robert Sneddon (Heinemann Library, 2001)

Eyewitness Guides: Energy, Jack Challoner (Dorling Kindersley, 1998)

Green Files: Future Power, Steve Parker (Heinemann Library, 2003)

Pachamama: Our Earth – Our Future (Evans Brothers, 2002)

Renewable Energy, Chris Oxlade and Nigel Saunders (Raintree, 2004)

Science at the Edge: Alternative Energy Sources, Sally Morgan (Heinemann Library, 2002)

Science at the Edge: Global Warming, Sally Morgan (Heinemann Library, 2002)

Sustainable Human Development: A Young Person's Introduction, Peace Child International (Evans Brothers, 2003)

Index